LAGOM

Avoid Waste and Live a More Fulfilling Life by Adopting the Swedish Lifestyle Choice of "Just Enough"

CLARA OLSSON

TABLE OF CONTENTS

Introduction

We have all heard of Hygge the Danish concept of comfort, but how many of us are aware of the Swedish concept of Lagom?

Few of us that's for sure, but Lagom is about to be the next big lifestyle choice for many of us feeling trapped by excessive consumerism and waste.

Let's face it we lead very wasteful lives; we throw food away at a tremendous rate. Even our relationships have become wasteful and ever easier to move on to the next one without having to put the work in that previous generations seemed to do.

In this book we will look at how we can use the concept of "the right amount is best" to make our lives easier and less wasteful. We will look at how we can apply Lagom to all the important aspects of our lives from our homes to our relationships and lots more in-between.

So slip out of your Danish Hygge for a brief period and embrace living with "Just Enough" Swedish style!

So What Is Lagom?

Lagom, pronounced Lar-gohm, is a Swedish word that translates to 'just the right amount'. In a less literal sense, lagom refers to a lifestyle which strives for a balance between work and rest, expense and frugality.

People who embrace the lagom lifestyle seek a middle ground of owning just enough, but not too much and working hard enough for life to be fulfilling, but not to the extent that life is stressful. Lagom also involves finding the correct mental balance and peace; a balancing act between enjoying life but also working hard and managing responsibilities.

Lagom is also associated with the concept of fairness, sharing, and equality. In its most basic form, it is thought that sharing what you have will make you happier. This is not only because giving to others makes us happy, but it also encourages others to give to us in return – everyone benefits.

Naturally, lagom also involves concepts of environmental sustainability and ecological awareness. Fundamental concepts such as not living beyond your means and sharing are applied to nature itself, encouraging society to take care of the planet and avoid needless waste or damage.

As the world becomes more globalized, societies in the West have demonstrated a growing concern in the philosophies and lifestyles of other cultures. Lagom offers an alternative to the exotic and grossly misinterpreted ideas from the East; instead of advocating a simple, secular and straightforward approach to happiness and health.

In fact, the lifestyle changes associated with lagom are changes you've probably already considered or at least been recommended.

They include recycling more, saving energy, wasting less water, eating healthily, ensuring you always eat breakfast and so on. Whilst each of these changes might not produce a large effect on their own, together they can start to create a rich and easy-going lifestyle which benefits not only you but also everyone else too.

Origins of Lagom

Although usually translated as 'in moderation', the word Lagom has no direct equivalent in English. In general, many Swedish words contain denser, richer meanings than their English equivalents and it can be quite hard to translate the subtle nuances and unique flavors of the language.

Several countries have words with a similar meaning, but for the Swedes, the word Lagom carries a special importance – it is a concept to live your life by.

According to myth, the word Lagom originates from historic Viking practices. When drinking together, people in Viking society would drink from the same horn or bowl. In order to ensure that everyone gets a good swig, the concept of 'laget om', a fair portion, developed.

Laget om can also be understood as 'enough to go around', evoking the concept of sharing and social responsibility that is also found within the modern concept of Lagom. Over time, laget om supposedly evolved into lagom and the notion of moderation in all things.

Etymologists reasonably disagree with the Viking story. More realistically, the word lagom is derived from the root word 'laghum' which means 'according to law'. Of course, whilst living according to the law is undoubtedly part of Lagom, the idea of Lagom has become so much more.

Although it can be considered a lifestyle or a principle, Lagom can be used in general conversation. When a Swedish person asks how you are, *Lagom* is an appropriate answer, similar in feeling to 'great', 'just right' or 'perfect'.

Lagom can also be used to describe the weather, or when something seems to hit the right spot (such as describing a good meal).

LAGOM AND YOUR HOME

To truly embrace Lagom, you're going to need to change the way you think about your house and the stuff you buy. Lagom involves a personal responsibility to the planet, but being environmentally friendly can also help save your wallet.

To start with, try replacing old lights with environmentally friendly alternatives. Most households use incandescent light bulbs – the traditional pear-shaped bulb that we imagine lighting up when someone gets an idea.

However, these light bulbs are notoriously inefficient; most of the electricity they receive ends up producing heat instead of light. Furthermore, incandescent light bulbs have a short light span and typically only last between 1-2 years.

Replacing incandescent light bulbs with *light emitting diodes* (LED's) or *Compact Fluorescent Lights* (CFL's) is more efficient and better for the planet. These light bulbs last much longer and convert a greater amount of electricity in light, instead of wasteful heat.

As a result of being more energy efficient, over their lifespan LED or CFL bulbs will save you a significant amount of cash in the form of lower energy bills. LED's or CFL's also have other advantages; they tend to be harder to break, available in a wider variety of sizes, provide a better spread of light and produce a more natural, warm light.

Of course, regardless of whatever light bulbs, you are using, you can also do your part for the planet by turning off your lights whenever they are not in use. Try to develop the habit of flipping the light switch off whenever you leave a room and making sure all household lights are off before you go to bed or leave the house.

Moving away from household lighting, you should also think carefully about what you buy. Favor products which are not over-packaged with excess plastic or wrappings. Some supermarkets are particularly wasteful in their packaging, going so far as to wrap fruit in plastic, or individually wrap bread buns in their bag. Vote against such ridiculous practices by shopping elsewhere or favoring brands which show some common sense and only use packaging whenever necessary.

Likewise, shop in a way that makes it easy to recycle and reuse. Look out for products which are wrapped or stored in recyclable materials that are collected by your local area.

Even if your neighborhood has limited recycling facilities or collections, you can still re-use materials from the products you buy – good quality coffee jars, for example, make great storage containers for many types of food, such as rice or beans.

Similarly, try to plan your life in such a way that you can make use of products with longer life spans. For example, instead of buying a bottle of water or juice every time you are thirsty, invest in a higher quality, reusable water bottle that you can keep in your bag. It's not only environmentally friendly, but it's more convenient and will quickly end up saving you money.

Planning, in general, is a great way to live a lagom lifestyle. Even though there are many people and societies that struggle to feed themselves, modern reports show that nearly 50% of all food is wasted.

Of course, much of this waste is the fault of large industries for being inefficient, but it also takes place in most modern households. People rarely plan their meals in advance; they let fresh food spoil and end up just throwing it away.

Be grateful and respect your access to food, as well as the environmental impact it takes to create, by not allowing this to happen in your home. Plan what meals you want to have in advance and think carefully about your portion sizes.

Whenever possible, also favor frozen or canned alternatives to some fresh foods; they not only last longer, but they tend to be cheaper and can be bought out-of-season this way. If you prepare more food than you need for a meal, make an effort to wrap it up and use it later – you can cut down on the number of meals you need to cook this way too.

Additionally, consider the energy efficiency of all your household gadgets. If you are going to buy a new refrigerator, freezer, washing machine, dishwasher or any similar appliance, seek out the best energy efficiency rating possible; ideally, you want A+.

In terms of water use, you don't have to cut down on how often you shower. However, if you are someone who enjoys a couple of large baths every week, consider limiting yourself to just one. Baths use up so much more water than a shower and having multiple baths per week can really add up.

You can make an effort to be conservative with how long you leave the tap running too – for example, most people are wasteful and will leave the water tap running whilst they brush their teeth. That's several litres of water, wasted, for no real reason. You only need to turn the tap on briefly to wet your toothbrush, then once more to wash away the foam.

Dishwashers, washing machines, garden sprinklers and washing the dishes also contribute to our water use and you can probably make simple changes to make all of these more efficient. To start with, water sprinklers are massively inefficient – most of the water they spray will simply evaporate and they usually cover a much larger area than needed.

Furthermore, most people who use water sprinklers generally leave them active for much longer than they need, gorging on their water supply. If you need to water your garden, you can do so with a water bucket or garden hose, allowing you to give your plants just the water they need.

If you simply cannot part from your water sprinkler, do some research and learn how much water your plants actually require. It's probably much less than you think and you will only need to keep your water sprinkler active for just a few moments.

As for dishwashers and washing machines, just try to be efficient in how you use these appliances. Load your dishwasher properly; ensuring that you can clean as much as possible in one rinse and nothing needs to be re-washed. If you only need to wash a few plates or dishes, wash them by hand in a smaller sink or tub of water, as this is more water-efficient.

Lagom, Stimulation and Living Life in Moderation

In general, society teaches us to constantly search for new things. We move on to a new, hit T.V series after we have finished watching the last one on Netflix and we buy a new album only to become bored with it after listening to a few times. We are always on the lookout for tastier foods to eat, or new clothes to wear or new things to do.

Our gradual lack of interest in the things around us is due to how our brains react to stimulation. The first few times we perceive a stimulus our brains sharply focus on whatever stimulus we are perceiving, whether it be something we are watching on T.V or something we are eating and it gives us a short, brief, mental high.

However, after perceiving that stimulus half a dozen times or so, we become accustomed to it. Eventually, our brains start to pay less attention and get less pleasure from concentrating on it. As a result, we start to enjoy perceiving the stimulus less – we become bored and no longer gain any pleasure from the activity.

Watching T.V. and browsing the internet are two of the best examples of this effect. Any program or show we watch on T.V is full of scenes and events that are constantly changing, hooking our brains to keep watching by triggering a stimulation reaction.

If you've ever felt that the T.V or show you are watching has a hypnotic pull on your mind, or that you find a background show hard to tune out, this is the reason why – the physiology of your brain is working against you.

Browsing through the internet has a similar effect. The internet is full of interesting and novel stimuli; from a constant newsfeed stream from Facebook to hordes of endless YouTube videos or massive websites such as Reddit, it's easy for the mind to get hooked on all the novelty.

However, somewhere along the way, you might realize that you are not really enjoying yourself – you are only spending time on the T.V or the internet out of habit or instinct and that you are actually feeling quite bored or flat.

You might even want to pull yourself away or do something else, but be struggling with the motivation to do so.

There are two ways you can choose to respond to this ac- customization effect. The first method is to constantly seek new things and new experiences, which is the choice most people in Western society make by default.

Boredom is avoided by ditching the old and chasing novelty, wherever it might be. However, this approach has its limitations. There is a certain sense of desperation is constantly seeking new fleeting distractions from an otherwise boring or non-pleasurable life.

Like any addict, there is also an escalation effect – whatever we seek has to be more interesting and more engaging than the previous novelty, which eventually leads to us struggling to find something that genuinely interests us. Depending on your circumstances, you might also lack the means to constantly chase new things; the time and money just might not be available to try and keep your life feeling vibrant.

The second method is to learn to live in moderation and seek activities which are fulfilling by themselves. This approach is two-fold. By living in moderation and limiting the amount of time spent consuming media or doing 'entertaining' things, the acclimatization effect doesn't occur.

Our brains don't become accustomed to the things we do because we spend less time doing them. As a result, for the person who lives in moderation, when they do spend time watching T.V or browsing the web, they genuinely enjoy the experience – it still seems fresh and interesting.

The key here is balance – the person who lives in moderation might spend some time watching T.V, but they will only tune into the things that they are genuinely interested in. This type of person might watch a series like Game of Thrones, for example, looking forward to a new 1-hour episode per week. They are less likely to just watch T.V for the sake of it – browsing through hundreds of channels in the evening and settling for whatever seems the least boring.

The other half of this two-fold approach is seeking activities which are genuinely fulfilling. Instead of spending time on activities which we think are fun, but we typically admit bring us no real benefit (i.e. watching T.V.). A person who lives in moderation also adds things to their life which are inherently rewarding (such as learning a new skill, building new relationships or exercising).

Our interest in these activities doesn't fade over time – if anything these hobbies become richer and rewarding with the time we spend doing them. Above and beyond spiritual platitudes, the way our brains react to these types of activities is genuinely different – instead of getting a momentary high from perceiving something new, our brains enter a 'flow' state, associated with increased concentration, greater energy and a sense of joy and creativity.

Likewise, spending time on your hobbies and other activities which generate a flow state or you find fulfilling is also associated with greater happiness in general. Research suggests that engaging with hobbies makes you more confident and more independent because it teaches you that you can achieve things in your life outside of your work.

There is often an excuse that we don't have time for hobbies, or anything outside of work and our responsibilities, but for most of us, if we challenge ourselves, we know this isn't really true. It feels as if we don't have time because we are so used to wasting our time doing things we don't really enjoy, that we never feel rested.

Often, the people who claim they don't have time for anything are the same people who spend four hours watching T.V every evening – they are so used to this routine that doing anything else feels like an effort. Yet a little effort can go a long way; if you break out of the habit of squandering your spare time, you might find your life is not only richer and more rewarding but that you also have more free time to do other things.

There are a few other habits and techniques you can embrace to help you live Lagom. Firstly, try spending time doing activities that are slow and that deepen your concentration. Western society is developing a love affair with meditation for this reason, but you don't have to sit cross-legged to recapture your attention. Anything that makes your mind work a little slower than its normal pace is good.

Our minds are used to quickly flicking through new stimuli, largely due to the nature of our fast-paced T.V shows, smart phones, and internet distractions and perhaps the speed expected of us during our working hours. As a result, some psychologists have suggested we are losing our ability to pay attention to anything for more than just a few seconds at a time – an effect that is clearly detrimental to our ability to develop hobbies and find fulfilment.

So make an effort to deliberately fight this trend with anything that lets your mind slow down. Spend time walking outdoors in nature, reading a novel, painting or simply pausing for a moment to be mindful and aware. One blossoming example of a simple activity that can deepen your concentration is using a coloring-in book – in the past few years the sales of coloring books aimed at adults have exploded – in fact, at one point, demand was so high that there was a shortage of coloring pens!

Filling in the blank spaces in a coloring book is incredibly simple and easy; anyone can do it, even if they are tired. Nonetheless, it requires you to focus your attention on one activity for a long period of time, which is a fantastic way to deepen your attention span and recapture your concentration.

Another method to find balance is to delay gratification. You can still enjoy luxuries, treats, and pleasures but the ability to control our impulses by delaying gratification is paramount. When we delay and restrict the things that give us pleasure, we enjoy them even more. For example, if you eat chocolate every day, you might enjoy it, but not nearly as much if you only ate it once a week or once a month. When eating something every day we become bored and used to it, but when eating it once a month, the sensation is more intense and fuller.

Delaying gratification doesn't just apply to food, but to any pleasure you find yourself doing. If you have a couple of T.V series you really enjoy watching, such as Breaking Bad or Game of Thrones, try waiting to watch them on the weekend instead of immediately after you get home in the evening. It will give you something to look forward to and you can allow yourself to fully relax, knowing that the time you have devoted to watching your programs is not needed for anything else.

Finally, the last suggestion for finding Lagom is to focus on savoring whatever you are doing. If you are eating, focus on the flavors and textures of the food. If you are watching T.V., put away any distractions and pay full attention to what you are watching.

When you spend time with other people, engage in the conversation – don't just take their presence for granted. Savoring your current activity this way generally requires you to stop multitasking constantly. Put the smart phone down and don't eat whilst you watch T.V, study or work, or listen to music as you browse the web. Instead, do things one at a time, but take care to enjoy each thing as you do it.

By focusing on the activity you are doing, especially if it's enjoyable, you enrich your experience of things. You will feel more rested, relaxed and calmed because you are paying more attention to the experiences in your life that are pleasurable and rewarding.

Lagom and Financial Stability

Finding the correct balance in life involves more than just your mental health – it is also about your finances and how you choose to spend your money. People who follow the Lagom lifestyle understand that it's okay to spend and splurge on occasion, but that clever frugality will provide you and your family with security and stability in your lives.

One way to achieve the correct balance is simply to be frugal in dozens of small, easy ways allowing you to save money for the more important events in your life. For example, if you are someone who buys your lunch at work, try preparing it in advance instead. A decent lunch can easily cost you $5 and this quickly adds up – that's $25 over five working days, $100 for a typical month and $1000 over the course of a year. That's the amount of money that could be used for something important; investments, car repairs, holidays, etc.

Fortunately, there are many, many ways to be frugal. To start with, try buying your staple foods in bulk and planning meals in advance, which is cheaper. Cooking meals in batches, then freezing or preserving these meals will be much more efficient than preparing meals individually and you can avoid spending money on snacks or fast food when you don't want to cook in the evening – just heat up a meal you have already made!

Perhaps more importantly, another way to save you money is to avoid paying interest whenever possible. Loans and delayed payments are almost always awful ideas as they end up costing significantly more than the actual price of the good. For expensive goods, such as cars, electric appliances or furniture delaying that payment of $1000 over several months, or even years, might seem immediately appealing.

However, why pay more for something than what it is actually worth? The interest on these types of payments will keep you cash-starved for months and years to come, which in turn can force you to rely on loans and delayed payments in the future. With wise spending, most payments with interest are completely unnecessary, so avoid these financial traps whenever you can.

On the same vein, if you have any debts your first priority should be to pay them off. Any money you save through frugality will be going to waste if you are just leaking money through debts and interest already.

Another great piece of frugal lagom advice is to understand when it's the correct choice to pay more for an item and when it's the right choice to look for a cheaper alternative. For certain items, paying for high quality will save you money, as better quality items can last for longer and break less often.

Shoes are a popular example – cheaper shoes can be a ½ the cost of a more expensive pair, but soon the laces will start fraying, the sole will wear through and the interior lining will tear. In the end, you will need a replacement at least twice as fast, often costing you more in terms of cash and convenience.

As a general rule of thumb, for anything that can last for several years, or even decades, it's worth paying a little extra for better quality. This category includes items such as kitchen equipment and cutlery, workman's tools, any safety equipment and important pieces of clothing, such as suits, cocktail dresses or good-quality winter coats.

On the opposite end of the spectrum, it's often the right choice to look for the cheaper option when it comes to consumable items. This includes most foods and toiletries. Milk is milk, regardless of whether it costs $1 or $3; often you are just paying more for the 'brand' even when the product is exactly the same.

Likewise, items such as soap, shower gel, toothpaste can also be bought at a discount. It's true that there might be some nasty cheap brands, but you if you try a few different options you will find that in most circumstances, there's something just as good, if not better, than the brand you are used to for a fraction of the price.

Of course, it might seem harmless to spend an extra dollar on milk, but as touched on before, over the course of months or years it's these small expenditures that add up. You can buy more expensive milk, or you can save for a holiday or pension; the latter will undoubtedly have a bigger impact on your life!

Additionally, look to buy used items rather than brand new items whenever possible. Books, albums, electronics, furniture and clothes are all great candidates to get second-hand; if you look for bargains you can get items in good condition for a fraction of what it costs in retail. In most situations, people are selling these items to because they don't have room, or they need a little extra money themselves rather than the item being broken or damaged.

Many people, of course, already understand the various ways they may be able to save money. The difficulty comes, however, at applying this knowledge. You might know it's in your best interest to save some money, but if you see that dress in the shop you might not be able to help yourself. Bad habits can be hard to eradicate and many of us find ourselves spending money on junk, even though we know better.

Fortunately, there are a variety of techniques you can use to keep yourself from spending too much. For a start, whenever you go shopping to a mall or supermarket, only bring a limited amount of cash with you; leave your credit card at home.

If you only bring enough money for what you intend to buy, then you physically cannot spend the money on extra stuff that you see around. Of course, it's still wise to have a small margin of error and bring just a little extra money, just in case something goes wrong. Nonetheless, by limiting yourself you can make it much harder to spend too much.

On a related note, always plan in advance what you want to buy. This means you can plan your route around a supermarket or shopping mall quicker, just navigating to the items you intend to purchase and reducing the temptation to peruse the other isles. Noting want that you intend to buy also helps you stay focused as you shop and makes it harder to justify impulse buys along the way.

Whenever you want to buy something that you don't immediately need (such as some tinned food or medicine) try waiting 1 month before making the purchase. If you are still thinking about the item after 1- month, you probably genuinely want it. If you forget the item (as you most likely will) it probably wasn't that important in the first place.

Above and beyond your capacity to remember things, waiting a little while before making a purchase is a good way to allow your emotions to settle. Even if you remember that you intended to make a purchase, chances are you might feel differently about the item if you wait a while. You'll probably realize that you didn't want it as much as you thought you did and that you are glad you didn't buy it straight away. Alternatively, you might also realize that there is a better choice of product that comes along.

Avoid keeping your credit card details saved on apps and websites. Platforms such as Amazon make it easy to buy anything with just a single click or tap; they remember your bank information and simply charge your account with the tab.

For people who know they spend too much, this makes life uncomfortably easy. With no barrier or effort in place to deter you from spending, it can be too tempting to say no. Avoiding platforms like Amazon might be the best option, but at the very least, you can change your account settings so that online marketplaces don't remember your credit card details – this forces you to go to the effort of entering them every time you want to make a purchase, which can help to limit your impulse buys.

It can also help to go shopping with someone who has a better handle on their spending habits. If you know you spend too much, try taking a spouse or friend with you when you shop, as their presence or judgment might help keep you in check. Of course, on the opposite end of the spectrum, if your friends or family members are bad influences, ensure that you shop alone and don't let them encourage you or spend time shopping that you don't need – there are many other things you can do!

Lagom, Clutter & Minimalism

The lagom lifestyle seeks to find the goldilocks sweet-spot in every area of its life; not too much and not too little. If you look around your house right now, you'll probably realize that this concept doesn't apply to your surroundings.

Most people are hoarders, accumulating far more possessions than they could ever want or need. Even without all the excess clothes, books, ornaments, films, games, toys, shoes (and so on), most people still have far too much furniture. There is a beauty and elegance in having an emptier room with just a few key pieces of furniture. A minimalistic room is calming, pleasant to be in and easier to keep tidy and clean.

So, to truly live lagom, it's time to start getting rid of the clutter. A lot of people struggle deeply with separating themselves from their possessions, so it can be best to be slow and gentle in your approach when trying to separate yourself from your stuff.

Start by dipping your toes in the water and getting rid of any duplicate possessions. Often you might realize that you actually own multiple copies of the same book or film or that you own a bunch of clothes that all fulfil the same purpose.

Do you really need five pairs of gloves or six scarves? Likewise, if you comb through your kitchen, you'll probably recognize that you probably have too many frying pans, saucepans, cutlery or other equipment. Not only do you have too much, when you start to think about it, you'll probably realize that you only use just a few pans or plates and that you keep everything else around for the sake of it.

Another easy way to trim down on the clutter is to get rid of anything that is broken or faulty, especially if it's not required. Our sense of wastefulness encourages us to keep things until they are completely non-functional, but if you're not using it, then it's just getting in the way. This category includes things such as socks with holes, saucepans with broken handles, power tools that are no longer working and clocks which no longer tell the time. Make a concrete decision; either devote time and money to getting the item repaired, or let it go.

If you can cut down on your clutter using these two techniques, then you've made a good start, but there is usually so much more you can do!

Tackle the attic or garage, filtering through all the boxes you've put there to deal with sometime 'later'. Try to sort items into four categories; keep, sell, give and discard. Often junk ends up being stored just because we are too lazy to get rid of it at the time – we would rather just store something away than deal with it right there and then. Of course, this approach backfires on us; we not only have to deal with the junk later, but it takes up space in the meantime and can get in the way when we need to find something.

Anything that you don't want to keep but is too good to throw away is something you should be selling, or at the very least, giving away. Don't be lazy!

Selling things in the modern era isn't hard with the internet making the process only take a few moments. If you plan to sell, all you need to do is make a listing on a website such as eBay or Amazon. Take a few good quality photos of the items you are selling and make sure to include them in your listing. In the photos, the item needs to be visible, in bright light, from a few different angles and preferably against a blank background (and clean, mono-color area of carpet or surface will do).

Add a short, but clear and honest description of the item and then set a reasonable price. For someone to buy your item, it's going to need to be at an attractive price, but you should still be able to make a few dollars on most items worth selling. Be careful to think about the cost of postage in your price – you'll probably only want to sell to places within your country and you should look up the prices and dimensions of parcels to make sure you are charging enough to cover the costs and still make a small margin of profit.

Some items are unlikely to be sold for any real value. Most books are far too common and too cheap, to be worthwhile selling on most platforms. Likewise, larger objects such as most pieces of furniture will be too expensive and bothersome to ship anywhere and make money.

However, most charity shops and organizations are more than happy to take any quality goods off your hands for free, provided you are willing to move the items yourself. Through platforms such as Craigslist, or even popular social media groups on websites such as Facebook or Instagram, you can advertise that you are giving away stuff. If you include a good description, contact details, and a few good photos, you'll soon get a lot of interest – people like free stuff!

At this point, some people will feel successful in their attempts to de-clutter. However, for some people decluttering is more than just getting rid of junk, duplicates, and broken stuff. For these people, decluttering also involves learning how to use and need less altogether; developing a lifestyle that revolves around fewer possessions.

However, Lagom is not austerity or a rejection of material things. Lagom is about living in moderation and achieving the correct balance of not too much or not too little. What is considered 'just enough' will vary person by person and for some people, this might simply involve having more possessions than others.

Nonetheless, it can be revealing to challenge yourself to look at all your possessions and think about which ones you truly need and which ones truly make you happy. If we are honest with ourselves, you probably own a huge amount of stuff that doesn't contribute to your happiness and nor is it stuff that you actually need. Look at your house right now. What do you use on a weekly basis? What do you use on a daily basis? What would you notice missing if it suddenly disappeared?

If you suspect that you don't really need something, but you're not willing to fully let it go, try storing it away for a month. If you forget about the item or realize that didn't need to use that item for the entire month, then you probably don't need it. At the very least, it probably isn't contributing to your happiness in any meaningful way.

One popular application of this concept has become known as the 'capsule wardrobe'. The capsule wardrobe involves limiting yourself to around 40 or so pieces of clothing, including accessories such as shoes or scarves. The capsule wardrobe is adjusted at the start if every season, with necessities such as warmer clothing being subbed in for summer clothing as the months grow colder. Everything else is stored away or sold.

Through the capsule wardrobe experiment, people are starting to realize that they actually only need very few items of clothing and a large wardrobe full of clothes is completely unnecessary. In fact, you probably already wear only a few outfits 80% of the time already, with everything else in your wardrobe being items that are worn rarely (such as a dress suit) or items that are not worn at all (such as items that are too big, too small, that you don't really like or have similar clothes that you prefer).

Interestingly, what makes the capsule wardrobe experiment so popular is how liberating it feels to restrict your options. People are finding themselves overwhelmed with the sheer amount of choices they have to make about what they wear on a day-to-day basis. By limiting yourself to a smaller collection of just your favorite pieces, the choice becomes easier, yet at the same time more meaningful. You start to enjoy thinking about what you want to wear in the mornings and taking a greater effort for your clothes to match and go together. The capsule wardrobe makes something as simple as what you wear every day an interesting and vibrant part of your life.

LAGOM & FOOD

How can you find Lagom in your diet? Western society is notoriously on the larger size, so we are clearly not achieving the right balance in how much we eat, but perhaps the very idea of Lagom can help us here.

In general, most diets are harsh and focus on an abstinence or deprivation of the foods we like to eat. This is clearly not Lagom! To truly live in moderation we need to embrace a slice of cake every now and then and be happy to gorge ourselves, on occasion. By failing to moderate our diets and trying to be too strict with our approach to health, we actually end up causing more damage through yo-yo dieting.

In psychology, there is a concept called which is literally called the 'what-the-hell effect'. It refers to that special moment where you break your diet by overeating or eating the wrong type of food. By breaking the diet, the dieter usually takes the opportunity to eat as much as possible, which often results in the individual consuming more calories than if they were not to diet at all.

Driving this response is that defeated feeling that if the diet is already broken, you might as well go 'all-out' and enjoy yourself, or sneak in as much junk food before you officially start your diet again. Alternatively, for those of us who are emotional eaters, the disappointment of breaking our diet may cause us to resort back to binge eating as a habitual way to cope with our feelings.

Of course, we typically feel that it's our fault for breaking diets and that we should just try again. However, perhaps a different approach might be more successful. Strong innate desires drive us to eat and resisting these urges is difficult. If you have struggled with your weight or diet before, try taking a more balanced approach; allow yourself unhealthy food every now and again, but just don't go overboard.

Instead of seeing a diet as a black and white set of rules and limitations, try interpreting with a dose of Lagom; it's okay to break the rules every now and again and it's better to let yourself have a few treats than breakdown and eat far too much.

It's important to note that the what-the-hell effect is not just limited to food but can be applied to various areas of your life, including money or telling the truth.

If you've set yourself a budget and break it, you are more likely to spend much more than you initially set out. Likewise, if you've made a pact to yourself, to tell the truth, and you let out a little fib, you tend to fall back into habitual lying. Susceptibility to the what-the-hell effect seems to be a personality trait; if you are more likely to fall prey to this effect in your diet then you are vulnerable in your finances and other aspects of your life too.

As a result, to live Lagom, it's important to set realistic goals. In terms of dieting, you could allow yourself one unhealthy treat per day, or one day of the week where you can eat anything you want. In terms of budget, you can set aside a fixed amount for frivolous spending per week.

Better yet, research demonstrates that it's better to set a specific type of goal, called an acquisitional goal. For example, if you wanted to lose weight, it would be better to set the goal that you want to lose 10 lbs rather than claiming you're only going to eat 1500 calories per day.

In both goals, the aim is clearly to lose weight. However, with the latter goal, it's easy to feel like a failure the moment you've exceeded that magical 1500 calorie limit. With the former goal, there is no direct way to fail; you can drift further away from achieving the goal, or take longer to achieve the goal, but as long as it's physically possible for you to lose that weight, then you can still succeed. By framing the goal in a way where failure isn't possible, you can avoid the pitfalls of the what-the-hell-effect.

Similarly, it's also wise to avoid goals which tell you to stop doing things. The concept of *not doing* something is difficult for the human mind to process – our minds are built to think about things rather than to not think about things. In fact, the very idea of not thinking about something is strange and difficult, to begin with. In psychology, this effect has been observed in a phenomenon called the 'white polar bear effect'.

The white polar bear effect was first noted in a simple experiment where researchers asked a group of participants to try and avoid thinking about a white polar bear. Naturally, by asking the participants to not think about the polar bear, people started to think about the polar bear immediately. In fact, the harder people tried to forget everything about white polar bears, the more they started to think about polar bears. Essentially, by trying to avoid or stop doing something, people can make themselves more susceptible to doing it.

In a more realistic example, consider being on a diet and trying to avoid eating the biscuits in the cupboard. You can say to yourself that you shouldn't eat the biscuits, but by thinking about the biscuits, to begin with, you are already tempting yourself. The more you think about the biscuits, the more you tempt yourself. You are setting yourself up to fail.

Instead of trying to not think about the biscuits, a better strategy is to think about something else. By distracting yourself, you can forget about the biscuits altogether and not be tempted in the process. Similarly, by setting yourself a goal to do something else, instead of inhibiting your actions, you also avoid the type of intrusive thinking that makes you susceptible to falling prey to your temptations.

So, for example, when you are hungry, instead of trying to avoid eating biscuits, or any type of junk food, try drinking a large glass of milk. Milk is quite filling, cheap and relatively low in calories – research has shown by drinking 400ml of milk in the morning, people tend to eat less throughout the day, therefore consuming fewer calories and losing weight. By setting the goal of drinking milk, you are not thinking about the biscuits at all, instead, you are thinking about milk, bypassing the temptation altogether.

This type of positive goal setting demonstrates the power of Lagom in action. It's not about heavily restricting yourself, but seeking a comfortable and better middle ground. On the same vein, if you do struggle, even with a positive goal don't be too strict on yourself and learn to forgive yourself when you break rules. More importantly, if you do break your diet, budget or any set of restrictions placed on yourself, understand that it's only a temporary setback. Getting too upset or too angry with yourself isn't Lagom; understand that it's okay to be disappointed, but you can still feel positive about the future too.

Lagom & Relationships

Humans are social mammals. Whilst some people are more sociable than others, very, very few people have the nature to live alone, without any contact. For the vast majority of us, socializing with others is a human need alongside food, water, and shelter.

Nonetheless, despite our sociable nature achieving Lagom in our relationships is difficult. Often people feel like they are suffocated and surrounded with people, yet somehow not finding any meaningful relationships. Alternatively, people often find themselves lonely, not forming bonds or spending enough time with people altogether.

The key to finding Lagom in relationships is to firstly understand your own personality and the difference between introversion and extroversion, which will help you, understand how you connect to people.

Introversion and extroversion are a spectrum, which in psychology, is defined by how much stimulation a person enjoys. Introverts are more sensitive to stimulation and therefore enjoy and thrive in lower-stimulation environments. As a result, introverts often enjoy spending time during low-key activities, such as reading, listening to music, or socializing with just a few close friends.

Of course, introverts can also enjoy more lively settings, but at the same time, find these activities draining. Someone with an introverted nature may enjoy going to a party or a concert but will find themselves feeling tired afterward and needing some time to relax in some low-key activities. Introverts recharge through low-stimulation activities, during which they feel most alive and awake, which are generally performed alone, but very good friends or family members can be involved too.

As a general rule of thumb, introverts tend to be more self-reflective. They reflect and dwell on their own mental states often and more likely to be concerned about how they are acting or thinking compared to extroverts.

It may be this self-reflective nature that makes social interactions more taxing; an introvert will be more likely to monitor their actions, thoughts, and feelings compared to an extrovert, which might make social interactions seem more daunting, whilst rewarding environments where introverts are alone or around people they feel comfortable with are more desirable and sought after.

Introverts enjoy focusing deeply on a single activity and they would rather observe or understand events from afar before joining. Introverts choose their relationships with much more care than others; they tend to have fewer friends and relationships, but these relationships typically involve a deeper bond with more trust involved.

Introversion is commonly associated with shyness, but this is a misunderstanding. Introverts can still be sociable, bold and confident. However, introverts typically approach social relationships slightly differently; their reflective and analytical nature can be mistaken as being withdrawn or simply not as warm as others. Shy people, by contrast, typically fear or avoid social situations, especially around new people.

In general, extraversion is more common and roughly two-thirds of people roughly fall into the extraversion category. As a result, some psychologists have suggested that society is biased against introverts, portraying that people who are sociable are more happy and successful and solitude is a negative, if not pathological, quality.

Extroverts are the complete opposite of introverts. Extroverts have a high tolerance for stimulation, which also means they enjoy, thrive and to an extent, need, more stimulating environments. Extroverts like environments where there are lots of people or lots of things going on and they rapidly become bored or frustrated when they are in their own company or if they are not occupied by doing something. Extroverts thrive when they are in groups and can find it harder to concentrate when they are on their own.

Extroverts generally have more friendships and relationships than introverts, although most of these friendships will be less intimate. With that being said, extroverts are more comfortable and confident in friendships and relationships which involve less trust, which they tend to still find enjoyable and rewarding. Extroverts also tend to be enthusiastic and talkative by default.

As touched upon previously, remember that introversion-extroversion is a scale and very few people fall far on a specific end of the spectrum, with most people being closer to the center than either extreme. Likewise, even for people who do fall into one end of the spectrum have exceptions to their behaviour; extroverts can still enjoy spending time on their own whilst introverts can still enjoy being in large groups.

Nonetheless, if you want to find Lagom in your relationships, it's important to understand where you fall on the introversion-extraversion scale. If you are an introvert, you might find yourself happier and more energetic cutting back on your social interactions and spending more time doing things you enjoy by yourself.

When you spend time by yourself, you might also find yourself enjoying your time more if you find yourself hobbies and activities you can focus deeply on - try writing, programming, or painting.

If you are an extrovert, it might be better to put yourself in situations where you can meet new people and occupy a greater portion of your week in company. Try to find hobbies which you can perform in a group or with friends.

After reading the previous section you probably have a good idea of where you fall on the introversion and extraversion scale, but nonetheless, it can help to ask yourselves the following questions:

- Are you comfortable being in large groups?
- Do you have lots of friends and know many people?
- Do you jump into things without thinking them through?
- Do you successfully plan what you intend to do before you do it?
- How often would people describe you as reflective?
- Do you enjoy spending time by yourself?
- Do you often feel like you dwell on things too long and don't take action?
- Do you often feel like you lack experience or are unfamiliar with the way the world is?

The first four questions look for examples of extraversion, whereas the last for questions look for signs for introversion. You'll probably find yourself learning one way, but you might also recognize signs of the opposite spectrum.

Of course, there is more to our relationships than just understanding our introverted or extroverted nature. In all relationships, whether they are romantic or platonic, there needs to be a balance in what people give to the relationship and what people take from the relationship.

Even if you enjoy someone's personality or company, you can still find yourself in a position where your relationship with them isn't rewarding – they take away much more from the relationship than they give you. Conversely, consider your relationships with friends, family, and partners; how much do you give in return for their attention.

Often, it's the small things that help a relationship feel more balanced. Make an effort to keep in contact, instead of presuming that the other person will keep in contact with you. Likewise, invite people to events and organize plans yourself, instead of being someone who waits around to be invited to things.

It feels awful to be the person who is always putting in the effort to make things happen without getting anything in response, so respect and treasure the effort people around you make by reciprocating it.

Additionally, be aware of the types of commitment that other people make for you and whether or not you are taking this for granted. This type of awareness includes paying your fair share for events you are involved in, but also displaying gratitude for favors, even for simple things, such as someone offering to drive you somewhere or sacrifice their time for you.

On top of this, consider how much attention you require and how much attention you give to people. Are you someone who always talks about your own problems, but doesn't listen to the problems of other people? Do you need to be the center of attention and struggle when other people are in the limelight? Do you only listen to people in order to have your turn to talk, or do you reflect and consider what they are saying? Do you always dictate the plans, or do you let other people have a say when arranging when you meet and what you do? These are all examples of being too self-centered in a relationship; you need to be genuinely interested in what the other person thinks, feels, says and acts. They don't just exist to make you feel good.

The balance of giving and taking needs to be right for both parties. You need to give enough to keep your relationships healthy, but you also need to maintain friends and family bonds where people don't take too much.

If you have friends that constantly ask you for favors, but don't give them, who are self-focused but don't care too much about your life and constantly require you to arrange plans, then consider whether the friendship is worth it for you. Even if you appreciate them as a person, or enjoy their company, in some circumstances you might be better off alone. At the very least it's worth trying to express your feelings and the ways in which you are not happy with the relationship – if the other person values you, they will make an effort to change.

Naturally, all relationships are difficult and the circumstance at hand might alter the balance of giving and taking. There is no perfect balance for everyone; what matters is how the people involved feeling about it.

Some relationships can be quite one-sided in terms of attention given, favors and sacrifices made and the overall sense of equality between people, but nonetheless still feels fulfilling and balanced to the people involved.

A wealthy individual might want to spoil their lower-income partner with gifts and treats for example, but this can feel inappropriate depending on the understanding and relationship these partners have.

Likewise, quieter and self-reserved person might enjoy spending time with someone who is louder and self-focused, achieving a type of asymmetrical balance.

Lagom & Work

Most cultures across the globe idolize working hard. The person who works long and difficult hours is seen as a person who is motivated, disciplined, and responsible. They are a go-getter who will climb the career ladder and they are not afraid of putting in the effort to get results.

All-in-all, working hard is seen as admirable and a longing for an easy or lazy life is perceived as a negative quality trait.

The Lagom lifestyle, however, understands that there needs to be the correct balance between your working life and everything else, a balance which is growing more precarious as Western workplaces are challenged by recessions, competitiveness, and globalization.

People can only work so hard for so long before the signs of wear and tear inevitably begin to show, with cracks in physical and mental health materializing. However, the drive and motivation to improve oneself, do a good job and not shy away from difficulty are all good traits too. We need to fall into neither extreme but find the best middle ground; Lagom.

But how can we tell if we are working too hard or whether we are just being a little lazy? One of the best ways is to consider whether the number of hours you work is preventing you from thriving in other areas of your life. Do you still find time to spend with friends and family? Do you have enough time to exercise and cook? Do you devote time to hobbies and crafts that you find rewarding? If you are answering no to these questions and the reason is a sheer lack of time, then perhaps you should think about making an effort to achieve a better work-life balance.

There are various steps you can take to this end. Firstly, it's important to communicate to your company when the demands are too much or too unreasonable. In larger companies, upper management may not be aware of the demands placed upon lower level employees, whereas in smaller, flexible organizations rescheduling or reorganizing workloads can be easier.

Overall, whilst it may be a dangerous choice in some hostile workplaces, you'd be surprised at just how often employers and employees can find a compromise in regards to working hours.

It can also help to think more carefully about how you work. Long working hours can be the result of inefficiency and poor planning, such as prioritizing the wrong tasks or simply taking too long to achieve something.

As the old adage goes, try to work smarter, instead of working harder. Seek better and quicker ways to accomplish the same result and you will find you have more free time for other things in your life.

Also, ensure that there is a clean cut between your working life and your home life. With the prowess of modern communication technologies, such as email and text-messaging, it can be difficult to distance yourself from the pressures of work.

Yet having some time in your life where you can relax without thinking about the problems in the office is key for good mental health. So try things like avoiding checking your emails in the evening, or refusing to take work-related calls during non-working hours. If you must work whilst you are in your home, try to designate a specific room as your office or study. It will be easier to get into a working mind-set whilst you are in that room, while also being easier to forget about work outside it.

If your working hours do limit your free time, ensure you sacrifice the right type of activities. Prioritize things which keep you mentally healthy and happy, such as exercise and friendships, over leisure activities that are more trivial (such as watching T.V).

Activities such as exercise or good social support function as protective factors, making you more resilient to the pressures of work and difficult, stressful events in your life.

On top of this, account for all the hours associated with your work. Even if you work eight hours in a day, an hour long commute both ways is still a commitment to your workplace. Likewise, tasks, such as delivering items, studying, research or working through lunch can all increase your workload, even if they don't fall within what you'd consider your normal working hours.

To help achieve Lagom in your work-life balance, you most first properly account for all the work you do.

Of course, you might find yourself on the opposing end of the spectrum; knowing you aren't working hard enough. Perhaps you are not working as many hours as you should be, or when you are working, you're aware that you are not putting as much effort into your tasks as you should be.

How can you force yourself to work as hard as you should be doing?

Firstly, you can surround yourself with people who work hard. Our relationships influence us and if you spend all your time around people who slack off, or lack motivation themselves, you can fall prey to their influence.

Seek role models and inspiration from the people you know and try to hold yourself to their standards.

However, regardless of the social circles you keep, you still need to fully convince yourself to work hard initially. You need to find a reason or a cause to justify working hard and this reason needs to be a strong internal drive.

You might only desire to work hard in order to earn more money, but by thinking about the reasons why you want more money can still lead to the motivation to push yourself. If you have a family you need to support, think about them and how much you care for the well-being and their needs. If you need or want money for yourself, consider what you plan to do with it, or how it could improve your life. Dwell on these reasons and let the emotions that fuel them come to the surface.

Lagom, Psychology, and Emotion

Perhaps the most important place to find Lagom is inside your own head. Even if everything else is right, it's impossible to be happy if you are trapped in cycles of negativity. It doesn't matter if you have every material need covered, family and friends at your side or even a pleasant lifestyle if you cannot find inner peace and balance.

The most important part of maintaining a healthy and happy state of mind is to realize that your thoughts and behaviour can be changed through effort and practice. Keeping positive is a skill, which takes time to learn, but when mastered, can be applied almost continuously.

On the contrary, negative thoughts and feelings can rapidly spiral out of control and become all consuming. Small irritations and frustrations, for example, can rapidly sour our day, even though in truth, they do not really matter.

We all know someone who is susceptible to road rage; someone who gets irrationally angry when they see someone driving too fast, too slow or in such a way that doesn't meet our high standards. As a result, the small task of driving anywhere can become a source of bitterness and anger that can last throughout the day.

You might not suffer from road rage, but most of us will have triggers that cause us unnecessary grief. We might dwell on how people are rude to us, how we are unhappy with our appearance, intelligence or our lack of popularity.

A simple negative thought can poison our mood and over time, they can contribute to illness such as depression and anxiety. Whilst most of us will experience some degree of personal difficulty throughout our lives, most people in the Western world are fortunate to be in a position where their needs are met; they are educated, safe and enjoy civil liberties.

We shouldn't brush aside genuine problems when they occur, but we should take it upon ourselves to recognize our good fortune and the trivial, superfluous nature of most of the difficulties we face on a day-to-day basis.

Although most of us will appreciate this wisdom to some extent, that doesn't make it easy to apply. There is a wide gap between how we know we should feel and act and the way we do, a gap that may be able to be crossed through intention alone. Therefore, we should make an effort to cross this gap through special techniques and tips, helping us achieve a wholesome state of mind.

To start with, try to develop a meditation practice. Small periods of mindfulness meditation have been demonstrated to help increase positivity, reduce stress and help battle depression and anxiety.

You don't have to try and find enlightenment, enter a trance or embrace any spiritual, religious or supernatural claims to benefit from meditation. Mindfulness meditation is simply an exercise in awareness and concentration, which can help us relax, energize and become aware of our thought patterns and behavior.

In mindfulness meditation, the meditator focuses on the breathing and the sensation of inhaling and exhaling the breath as it enters and exits the nose. Whenever a different thought or sensation arises, the meditator acknowledges it, becomes aware of the thought or sensation, and then returns to the breath. This way, the sensation of breathing functions like an anchor, helping the meditator to avoid becoming lost in thought or overwhelmed by emotion.

Generally, when practicing mindfulness meditation, most people become immediately aware of two things. Firstly, they recognize that their minds are very busy and that there is a constant stream of thoughts which serve no purpose.

Secondly, mindfulness meditation can also help reveal how limited our concentration and awareness is; it's hard to focus and clear your mind for even a few seconds.

Through returning the attention to the breath, the meditator can attempt to reach a state of calm, where the mind becomes less busy and their concentration deepens. Eventually, through learning how to reach a state of calmness and concentration, the meditator then is able to apply this state of mind to their lives, moderating their thoughts and behaviour and learning to recognize thoughts and actions that are harmful to them and those around them.

It's important that when practicing mindfulness meditation, that the meditator doesn't attempt to control the breath or its rhythm, but allows it to flow naturally.

The breath is such a fantastic focal point for awareness because it responds to our moods and feelings. If we are stressed or angry, the breath can become short, terse and painful. If we are relaxed and calm, the breath can become deep, free and soothing.

By focusing on the breath, not only can we become more aware of what we are currently feeling, but we can relax our minds and bodies through eventually allowing the breath to settle and become deeper of its own accord.

It's also important that you don't attempt to follow, dwell or chase any thoughts that occur. It's hard to translate or fully describe the difference between observing thoughts and feelings that pop-up and lingering on these thoughts, but most of us intuitively understand the difference.

Let the thoughts occur and monitor how your mind responds to them, but don't think about them any more than that. Imagine you are watching your thoughts flow down a river; you observe them as they pass, but you don't follow they flow downstream.

Meditation is usually performed in a position called the half-lotus position, where you sit on the ground or a meditation cushion and each foot rests on the opposing thigh. As a general rule, though, the position you attempt to meditate in is much less important than how much effort you apply or how consistently you meditate.

Any position that is comfortable, but also helps you stay focused and awake is desirable. Lying down in your bed is usually avoided for this reason – it makes it easy to fall asleep or simply daydream. However, many people perform meditation in kneeling postures or sitting down in an upright chair, so you can try different positions and see how they feel for you.

Meditation can be performed for any length of time. For people who are just beginning to practice, a small period of 15 minutes is generally the best option. 15 minutes is large enough to produce a difference in your mind-set but short enough to be easy to fit into your routine and not feel too challenging.

For meditators with more experience, meditating for longer periods can feel more rewarding and insightful and meditating in 45-minute sessions is common. In general, it's best not to get too hung up over how long you meditate; anything is better than nothing and meditating for longer is fruitless if you are not paying attention.

Finally, it's important that your meditation practice is consistent. Regardless of how long you chose to meditate for, meditating every day is important – just like it's important to maintain a good diet or exercise regularly, the benefits of meditation will only manifest if you meditate regularly. In general, it's best to meditate early in the morning when your mind is fresh and free from the thoughts and feelings that have built up during the day.

Whilst meditation can help you recognize negative thinking patterns, it can also help to research negative thought directly. Most types of negative thinking fall into common categories that are easy to recognize, also known as cognitive distortions.

For example, one very common type of negative thinking is called *filtering*. People who filter only acknowledge the negative details of a situation, and they magnify their importance, whilst ignoring the positive aspects.

Filtering is the opposite of seeing the world through rose-colored glasses and naturally leads to pessimistic and depressive outlooks on life and the world at large. A person who filters feels as if their life is overwhelmingly bad and bad things frequently happen to them – but this is rarely the case, but simply the result of not appreciating or being grateful for positive things.

Another category of negative thought it called polarized thinking, which is sometimes called 'black and white' thinking. In this cognitive distortion, you can only consider things being entirely good or entirely bad – there is no in-between.

As most events in life have positive and negative aspects associated with them, black and white thinking is linked with perceiving the world negatively. For example, imagine you had a pleasant evening out with friends. For a person with black and white thinking, the entire evening would be ruined if the meal was anything less than perfect or if someone arrived a little late – little flaws are allowed to spoil the entire thing.

In a more generalized sense, black and white thinking tends to make people feel bad about themselves and their lives. Instead of being able to perceive the positive and negative features of themselves, they will only perceive the negative features.

Catastrophizing, another negative thinking pattern, is not too dissimilar. People who display this thinking pattern anticipate disaster in every situation. They may avoid doing things or taking risks because of what-if thinking e.g. what if the car breaks down, what if they don't like me?

Other types of negative thinking patterns include *personalization,* where an individual feels as if they are to blame for everything that goes wrong and *emotional reasoning,* where you let your emotions dictate how you think about things.

Regardless of the name or category of the negative thinking pattern, all negative thoughts tend to follow the same overall trends – it focuses overly on the negative, discounts the positive, takes personal blame and generally is present far more often than it should be.

There may be times when it is correct to negatively appraise a situation, person or event but most people can frame these thoughts in a reasonable context.

For example, most people can recognize an undesirable quality in themselves (such as being slightly overweight) but also recognize positive qualities in themselves (such as intelligence or humor). Furthermore, a reasonable person also feels optimistic about the ability to improve and move forwards; a negative person tends to feel stuck in the same old habits.

The key to beating negative thoughts is learning to challenge them. This requires mindfulness of their presence, but also the inherent understanding that most negative thoughts are irrational or meaningless. Whenever you experience a negative thought about yourself, such as *I'm boring* or *I'm worthless* ponder the following questions:

- What evidence is there to support this thought?
- What evidence is there against this thought?
- Are there any other interpretations?
- Can the situation get better or is there a way this problem can be solved?
- What are the positives about yourself or the current situation?

If you are both honest and analytical, you will almost always realize that there is a brighter side to the situation that you are not considering. This doesn't mean that you deny how you are feeling, whether it is sadness, anger, desperation or any strong emotion, but simply that you can counterbalance these feelings with measured, realistic positivity.

CONCLUSION

The lagom lifestyle can be difficult to achieve, but its well worth the effort of trying. Seeking balance in all things can transform the lifestyle you already have, into a life that is fulfilling, rewarding and vibrant.

Lagom doesn't claim that you need to quit your day job and travel around the world to find happiness and nor does it ask you to embrace a shallow spirituality. Instead, lagom is found in the small things that make your life 'just right' - it's how you already live, just a little smoother, a little better, a little more lagom.

So whether it's doing your part for the planet, staying positive, owning fewer things or managing the turbulent world of relationships, hopefully, this guide can help you find that elusive and perfect middle ground; Lagom.

Made in the USA
San Bernardino, CA
11 October 2017